White House Butlers:

A History of White House Chief Ushers and Butlers

By Howard Brinkley

BOOKCAPS

BookCaps™ Study Guides
www.bookcaps.com

© 2013. All Rights Reserved.

Cover Image © Steve Cukrov - Fotolia.com

Table of Contents

ABOUT HISTORYCAPS 3

CHAPTER 1: INTRODUCTION 4

CHAPTER 2: THE EARLY YEARS OF WHITE HOUSE MANAGEMENT 9
    PAUL JENNINGS 13

CHAPTER 3: THE WHITE HOUSE CHIEF USHER 19
    IRWIN "IKE" HOOVER 22
    JAMES "J.B." WEST 35
    STEPHEN W. ROCHON 55
    ANGELLA REID 57

CHAPTER 4: WHITE HOUSE BUTLERS 59
    ALONZO FIELDS 60
    EUGENE ALLEN 80

CHAPTER 5: OTHER RESIDENTIAL STAFF 87
    EXECUTIVE CHEF 87
    GROUNDS SUPERINTENDENT 89
    SOCIAL SECRETARY 92

BIBLIOGRAPHY 98

About HistoryCaps

HistoryCaps is an imprint of BookCaps™ Study Guides. With each book, a brief period of history is recapped. We publish a wide array of topics (from baseball and music to science and philosophy), so check our growing catalogue regularly (**www.bookcaps.com**) to see our newest books.

Chapter 1: Introduction

Franklin Roosevelt said when he was president of the United States, "I never forget that I live in a house owned by all the American people and that I have been given that trust." Since George Washington selected its location on a hill overlooking the Potomac River and John Adams began living there in 1800, the White House in Washington, D.C. has been the home and office of the president of the United States.

The executive mansion has withstood torching by British troops in 1814 and a significant renovation that saved it from demolition in 1948. A stolen Cessna 150L airplane crashed on its lawn in 2004 while a magnolia tree planted by Andrew Jackson spared the house from harm. The White House has been the scene of numerous protests. Citizens, furious at John Tyler in 1841 for vetoing the attempt to create a Bank of the United States, burned an effigy of him. Women's suffrage activists held signs up for Woodrow Wilson. Anti-war activists shouted at Lyndon Johnson in 1968 as the Vietnam War grew more unpopular. Presidents and their loved ones have died while living there, Grover Cleveland's daughter was born there, children have run through its halls, dogs have romped on its lawns, and thousands of dignitaries from around the world have dined, danced, and slept there over the past two centuries.

Through it all, it has been the people behind the scenes that have ensured that the White House is ready for whatever each day may bring. When the White House first opened, there was no running water, so staff had to walk five blocks and haul water back to the president's home in buckets. When Benjamin Harrison and his wife, Anna, became the first White House residents to have the luxury of electricity in 1891, they were so afraid of getting shocked that White House staff had to flip the switches for them. Whether it is a white tie state dinner to welcome a foreign president or Susan Ford, daughter of President Gerald Ford, having her prom in the East Room, the residential staff make it happen. Even days that do not involve a special event can be busy ones. The staff is responsible for cooking, cleaning, gardening, maintenance, and whatever else needs to be done to allow the president to run the country.

While presidential administrations come and go, many people who work for the White House residential staff work there for 10, 20, or 30 years or more. They are loyal to the White House and its operations, not to a specific president. As a first family says goodbye to the staff, they have only a few hours before the next family moves in and they begin the process of serving a new president. Lillian Rogers Park, a seamstress and maid at the White House for 30 years beginning with the William Howard Taft administration, wrote in her memoirs, "When the old family goes out, you felt lost for just that flash. And then at 12 o'clock, when the other family comes in, you took on a new perspective. You just had to turn over; you had to forget those folks and start over."

One cardinal rule that the staff follows is to never tell an incoming president how the previous president liked things done. The staff make suggestions, if asked, but their first priority is to make sure the president is comfortable not only in the Oval Office, but in finding the makings for a midnight snack in the kitchen. Many people have worked to keep the White House functioning for the public that visits and for the families that live there. Maids, butlers, cooks, plumbers, gardeners, florists, and a whole host of other people call the White House their place of employment. As is the case for the president, they work as public servants on behalf of the United States. Unlike the president, they usually work with little recognition or fanfare.

Chapter 2: The Early Years of White House Management

Servants and Slaves

When Soviet leader Nikita Khrushchev visited President Dwight Eisenhower in 1959, he noticed several African American residential staff members. "Are these your slaves?" Khrushchev asked. In another era, they certainly could have been. Washington, D.C. is situated between Maryland and Virginia, two former slave states. Nine presidents from the South took some of their slaves with them when they moved into the White House. In fact, slave labor was used to help build the White House.

Even though he is the only president to never live in the White House, George Washington began the tradition of taking domestic help, including slaves, to the president's home. In Washington's case, it was in Philadelphia. Since Congress did not provide the funding for domestic staff, it made sense to the slaveowning planters who became president that they should bring slaves with them to Washington. The pre-Civil War White House generally had a mix of slaves, free African Americans, and white people to serve the president. However, John and Abigail Adams, the first residents of the White House, did not own slaves and had only a small staff of four. A steward, John Briesler, and his wife, Esther, were the primary staff members for the Adams administration, although the first lady said she could have easily found work for 30 staff members if only Congress would have paid for it.

Today, none of the residential staff live at the White House, although that was not always the case. Staff, including slaves, used to live in the basement and the attic. In fact, the second person ever born on the grounds of the White House was the child of two of Thomas Jefferson's slaves, Fanny and Eddy – the first was Jefferson's grandson, James Madison Randolph. Even though the White House had running water by 1833 and the president's quarters had a permanent bathtub with hot and cold running water by 1853, servants did not have access to running water for themselves until several years later. It was not considered a necessity yet and was only available to servants if it would help them work more efficiently, such as in the pantry on the main floor. When it came time to bathe, servants used portable tin tubs filled with water that they brought in from a well. Outhouses for servants were located off of the covered passages that connected the wings of the house.

Thomas Jefferson preferred to have white staff in the White House because he wanted to the ability to fire them if he was unhappy with their performance. Slaves served as butlers, maids, cooks, and other vital staff in presidential administrations through the 1850s. President James Buchanan wanted all of his staff to be from Great Britain because he felt they were better acquainted with the task of running a large house. The only exception was the butler, Pierre Vermereu, who was from Belgium. The last president to have slaves in the White House was Zachary Taylor, a native of Virginia who moved into the White House in 1849. In the years leading up to the Civil War, the issue of slavery was becoming more heated and not everyone was comfortable with seeing slaves in the presidential mansion. Therefore, Taylor's slaves primarily worked in the family's quarters on the top floor, out of the public eye.

Paul Jennings

As birthdates for slaves were not typically recorded, the exact date of birth for Paul Jennings is unknown. He was born sometime in 1799 on the Montpelier estate of James Madison, a Virginia plantation owner and the fourth president of the United States. When Jennings first stepped foot in the White House in 1809, he was 10 years old. His first impression of Washington, D.C. was that it was "dreary." Unusual for a slave of any age due to laws forbidding teaching them to read and write, Jennings was literate, and he later wrote his memoirs in *A Colored Man's Reminiscences of James Madison*.

He was also often in the presence of Madison and, an intelligent child, soaked up the information and knowledge from his surroundings. Jennings began as a footman, or male servant, to Madison. He was attentive but also understood his place, making him trustworthy in Madison's eyes. Jennings eventually became Madison's body servant and one of his responsibilities was shaving him, which he did for 16 years until the day Madison died in 1836. Most likely, Jennings also served as a waiter, porter, and postilion, who rides the leading horse of a horsedrawn carriage.

In the afternoon of an August day in 1814, Jennings set the table for a lavish dinner, due to begin at the usual time of 3 p.m. He retrieved ale, wine, and cider from the cellar and placed them in a cooler, following the orders of Dolley Madison, despite the fact that an invasion of British troops seemed imminent. Much of the city had already evacuated, but the first lady insisted that they maintain a sense of calm. Her resolve broke when word came from a free African American, James Smith, that the British had sailed up the Potomac and were on their way to the White House.

The first lady grabbed whatever silver she could and as she ran for a carriage, ordered the servants to break the frame and save the George Stuart portrait of George Washington that hung in the East Room. The large portrait, stretching 95 inches high, could not be saved easily. Jennings held a ladder while John Sioussat, a steward, and a gardener named Thomas McGraw, freed the portrait from the frame. The canvas was then rolled up and loaded into a wagon with other valuables. The portrait hangs in the White House today and is the only original object that remains from 1800. When peace was declared in 1815, the city was so rapt with joy that the servants were allowed to drink wine in celebration and Jennings broke out a rendition of "The President's March" on Madison's violin.

After Madison's two terms ended, he returned to Montpelier and Jennings accompanied him. He tended to Madison every day until his death. After Madison died, Jennings remained a servant to Dolley until she was forced to sell Montpelier. Not wanting to be sold with the property, Jennings negotiated, with the assistance of Daniel Webster, to purchase his freedom for the price of $120. Jennings paid Webster back by working for $8 a month until the debt was erased. While in Webster's employ, Jennings continued to look out for Dolley, who sunk into a life of poverty and ill health. He visited her often, taking baskets of food from the Webster household or, per Webster's instructions, anything else that Jennings felt that the former first lady might need. Jennings even gave her money out of his own pocket, made possible by the publication of his memoirs in 1865. When Jennings died in Washington, D.C. on May 20, 1874, he had outlived two of three wives, and he was a grandfather to 10 children.

On August 24, 2009, 15 of Jennings' descendants visited the White House and were taken to the East Room to see the Washington portrait that Jennings had helped save 195 years earlier.

Chapter 3: The White House Chief Usher

There have been only nine chief ushers since the position was established and given to Eldon Dinsmore in 1885, who famously stopped a crazed visitor from shooting President Chester Arthur. Prior to that, a male steward typically ran the White House. The White House chief usher does a lot more than answer the front door. J.B. West, who held the title from 1957 to 1969, said that the chief usher does whatever he is told to do. In many ways, managing the White House is like managing a hotel except that the only people staying there on a regular basis are the family members of the president of the United States. The person with this role is the head of all White House residential staff, is responsible for the budget for White House operations, helps coordinate official ceremonies at the White House, and oversees White House historical preservation.

The White House probably sees more activity today than ever before. After Gerald Ford faced two assassination attempts, it was decided that the president should not be so exposed to the public. Therefore, presidents have more activities at the White House than in prior generations. Now, it is a brief walk from the president's office to the event rather than a drive that would not only put the president at more risk, but also add to Washington's already legendary traffic problems. This has increased the duties of the chief usher and his or her staff.

Today, a chief usher is expected to have experience in managing large establishments, overseeing complex projects, and supervising various staff and departments. However, some of the earliest chief ushers happened to be in the right place at the right time to get the job offer and, in several cases, were reluctant to give the job up once they got it. Regardless of who has held the title of chief usher, they have all been required to perform their duties with the utmost discretion. Gary Walters, chief usher for seven presidential administrations, said that maintaining the privacy of the first family was probably his most important responsibility.

Irwin "Ike" Hoover

On May 6, 1891, 19 year-old Irwin "Ike" Hoover arrived at the White House to help install nearly 1,000 "incandescent lamps." Electricity had come to the White House, whether President Benjamin Harrison wanted it or not – and he didn't. He and his wife, Caroline, preferred the familiarity of gas lamps. Still, Harrison watched with curiosity as Hoover converted the chandeliers into combination gas and electricity fixtures and candle brackets on the wall were removed.

When Hoover finished the job on May 15, he assumed that his services were no longer needed. However, since Harrison was not comfortable with electricity, he decided that he should have someone working at the White House who understood it. The president offered Hoover the job of White House electrician, but Hoover hesitated before he accepted. The job paid a lower salary than he was making as a temporary employee at Edison Company. However, he did accept, and as he later said, became "a fixture," staying for 42 years. Hoover is such a part of White House history that it is difficult to read about Washington in the first half of the 20th century without seeing a mention of his name.

Among his first duties as electrician were to turn the lights off in the mornings because the president was too afraid to touch the light switches. In fact, nobody in the large contingent of Harrisons was comfortable with it, and Hoover said that a "family conference" was required just about every time one of them considering ringing the servant's bell. By 1904, Hoover had moved on from maintenance duties to usher while Teddy Roosevelt was in office. When William Howard Taft became president, Hoover was made chief usher.

The transition between Roosevelt and Taft was not an easy one for Hoover and his staff, who found William and Helen Taft to be far less easygoing and friendly than Teddy and Edith Roosevelt. Further complicating matters was that the first lady tended to ignore the fact that the White House is a public building. She immediately went to work transitioning the White House into the Taft family house. She preferred to have a housekeeper manage affairs rather than a steward. African American footmen replaced police guards at the door. Hoover and the rest of the staff were ordered around like servants and the staff grew to resent the Tafts. However, Helen had a stroke only two months after moving in, and she never fully recovered, so many of her planned changes were never carried out.

Among Hoover's duties during the presidency of Woodrow Wilson was to first keep secret that the president was having a romance and then, when it was no longer a secret, to arrange the president's marriage. Wilson's first wife, Ellen, died of liver disease in August 1914, about two years after the inauguration. He was devastated by her death and Hoover recalled the White House feeling sad and lonely without her. However, in 1915, Wilson met a fashionable, wealthy 42 year-old widow and suddenly Mrs. Edith Boiling Galt was to be included in White House social affairs. Wilson went so far as to consult the Library of Congress to find just the right quotes to express his feelings for her in his letters. Meetings were put off or cancelled altogether as Wilson soon began to spend nearly every waking minute with Edith. The staff was happy that the president had found new love, even if his immediate family was not, although the fact that war was raging in Europe certainly complicated the president's romance.

Wilson soon announced that he was marrying Edith Galt on December 18, 1915. Hoover was put in charge of the wedding arrangements, but the wedding ceremony was to be held at Edith's home, not the White House. He was glad to discover that she was perfectly willing to let him take charge of the planning because preparing for a state dinner always presented some challenges. He had planned the wedding for Wilson's daughter, Eleanor, who was married at the White House on May 7, 1914, just as he did for Teddy Roosevelt's daughter, Alice in 1906.

However, the president's wedding was new territory for everyone on the staff. Planning a wedding at a private residence that was so small that the band had to be located in the bedroom was utterly unprecedented. Still, Hoover oversaw every detail including arranging for caterers and florists, keeping track of the avalanche of wedding gifts that arrived within days of the announcement, and helping make plans for the president and his bride to get away for their honeymoon without the press finding out where they were going.

The ceremony came off without a hitch, and as the Wilsons left the Galt residence and climbed into a waiting car, Hoover got into the Secret Service car that was behind them. The president's car sped off, leading a parade of vehicles that gave chase. Hoover recalled that there were so many cars trying to follow the president that, for a while, he was not sure that the Secret Service car was following the right vehicle. However, they arrived at the train station shortly after the president and his wife did. An elated Wilson thanked Hoover for all that he had done before he boarded the train that took him and Edith to Hot Springs, Virginia for a three-week honeymoon.

Certainly there was more to Hoover's duties than planning weddings. He was one of the few staff members that went with Wilson to Europe at the end of 1918. Wilson went to France to discuss peace negotiations for World War I and while there, was one of many of people around the world to contract the flu virus in early 1919. Hoover was already by Wilson's side 12 to 14 hours a day and felt that the president was trying to keep up a positive front, even though the strain of the attention on him was beginning to wear him down. When he went to bed with what he called a cold one day, Hoover said that Wilson woke up the next day a changed man, and not for the better. He was no longer the healthy, robust man that he once was.

Later in 1919, Wilson had a massive stroke that left him paralyzed on his left side. Hoover tended to him constantly while he and Edith did all that they could to keep him out of the public eye. Unable to walk and barely able to speak, Hoover was saddened to see what Wilson had become. He was rolled in on a chair to cabinet meetings but barely participated. Cabinet members were kept at arm's length, and a select few had any idea how sick Wilson was. Hoover kept these details to himself until his book, *Forty-Two Years in the White House*, was published posthumously in 1935.

Ike Hoover's staff grew during the administration of Herbert Hoover. Like nearly all of the staff, Hoover considered this administration the most difficult he experienced. The president and his wife liked to entertain and did so lavishly, despite the fact that an economic crisis was brewing. They seemed to know more people and expect to entertain more people than any White House residents before them. While this did not demand any more of Ike Hoover's time, as he was accustomed to long hours, it did require more staff. The president and the first lady were quick with orders and demands and preferred to have people near them that agreed with them, rather than tell them the truth. To add to the tension, President Hoover was rarely away from the White House, so the staff never got a break from him. When the one-term president moved out, most were glad to see him go.

When Franklin D. Roosevelt arrived in 1933, Ike Hoover was among the first to greet him. The arrival of the Roosevelts totally changed the atmosphere of the White House as they were far less formal and demanding. Hoover also noted that seemingly overnight, "Republicans dropped out of sight." The fact that Eleanor said that hot dogs were to be on the Inauguration Day luncheon menu signaled that things were going to be different. Hoover recalled that Mrs. Roosevelt "knew what she wanted," but was still open to Hoover's suggestions.

On September 14, 1933, just six months into the FDR administration, Hoover left his small office at the White House and went home. He never returned to the White House because he suffered a fatal heart attack and died at the age of 62. Roosevelt said later that day, "It was Ike who met me at the door when I came to make the White House my home. It was good to receive his welcome and during these months to have his help and devotion in official and family life."

James "J.B." West

James "J.B." West was sent from the Veteran's Administration to the White House to work as an assistant to the proper Chief Usher Howell G. Crim in 1941. He was told that he met the qualifications because he could type, take shorthand, and mind his own business. On his first day, March 1, he met Eleanor Roosevelt, who he described as "an awesome study of human motion." He recalled that she never walked anywhere. She ran. Conversely, on his second day, he learned the magnitude of President Roosevelt's paralysis as he towered over FDR in his wheelchair. West was shocked to see that Roosevelt's legs were withered and useless.

West also gained a greater understanding after FDR died in 1945 about how the staff is loyal to the White House, not a president. During his time in the White House to that point, he had only known life with the Roosevelts. The abrupt changing of the guard as Harry Truman was sworn in was difficult for West at first. He wondered how Crim could so easily announce "The President of the United States and Mrs. Truman" when he escorted them to see Eleanor Roosevelt in the Red Room. Then he understood that even though Crim was as sad as anyone about Roosevelt's death, the government had to continue to function, and it was their job to make sure that the Trumans had whatever they needed.

Crim gave West, a native of Iowa, primary responsibility for serving the Truman family. The Trumans were from Missouri and Crim thought that West would have a better understanding of their needs. At his first meeting with Bess Truman, West liked her immensely. As many of the staff quickly learned, the Trumans were much more simple people than the Roosevelts. They did not want to be a bother to anyone and did not ask for much. Bess was direct, but kind and all of the Trumans treated the staff with respect. Each Sunday afternoon, Bess sent the maids home early, despite their protests that they might be needed. She replied that she was perfectly capable of turning down bed covers herself. West had to remind her when she asked permission to use a White House limousine that the cars were always available for her use.

One of the first things that West discovered about Harry Truman was that he was a man of routine. He was up at 5:30 every morning and headed out the door at 6 a.m. for a brisk walk, accompanied by Secret Service, no matter what the weather. West often passed him as he made his way to work at 6. From there, Truman met with a physical therapist, swam in the pool, and finished with a session in the sauna. A large breakfast was served promptly at 8 a.m. and the president expected Bess and their daughter, Margaret, to eat with him. Bess had a dry sense of humor and West recalled that often Harry and Margaret would howl with laughter while Bess held court over their morning meal. When breakfast ended, Truman went to work. He took a nap every afternoon at 2 p.m. and had cocktail hour with Bess when the workday was done. After a family dinner, staff could hear the sounds of family life such as Margaret and her friends singing or Bess reading to her mother, who also lived at the Whit House. Every night at 9 p.m.,

Harry and Bess retired to his study to work on his speeches or discuss politics. Bedtime was at 11 p.m.

The Eisenhower Administration brought more change to West and the White House residential staff. Mamie Eisenhower was a general's wife and ran the White House as such. The staff came to be known as "Mamie's Army." She told West that whenever she left the White House she was to be escorted by an usher and when she returned, she should be met at the door and escorted upstairs. When she discovered that her husband had approved a luncheon menu, she said that she was in charge of everything in her house, and she would approve all menus in the future.

Beginning in 1954, West split his duties between the White House and the Eisenhower family home in Gettysburg, Pennsylvania. He considered working on the rambling country estate his favorite task for the Eisenhowers. His job was to supervise the house's renovation and Mamie made it clear that she did not want any contractors in the home unless either she or West was there to supervise. When the renovation was complete, the Eisenhowers spent almost every weekend in Gettysburg and took several staff members with them. West oversaw this, too, ensuring that linens were packed and shipped out for cleaning every day, as well as supervising the transfer of food from the White House refrigerator to the refrigerator in Gettysburg.

West found himself at Gettysburg nearly around the clock for a period of time in the fall of 1955. President Eisenhower had a heart attack while visiting family in Denver and Mamie told West that she wanted all of the work on Gettysburg complete by the time that the president returned there. Eisenhower spent the last two months of 1955 in Gettysburg, recuperating and deciding if he should run for a second term. Ultimately, he did run and was re-elected. Shortly after that, Crim removed himself from the chief usher position due to poor health. While Crim spent his final year in the White House as a special assistant to the president, West was promoted to chief usher.

As chief usher, West was responsible for coordinating one of the most important visits of Eisenhower's second term. Queen Elizabeth and Prince Philip, along with a party of 15, visited the White House in October 1956. Mamie was insistent that their stay be an elegant affair unlike any before. She had visited the Queen's parents in her younger years and wanted to return the grand hospitality she had received. The highlight of the visit was a state dinner for 200, complete with an orchestral concert and a champagne reception. The Queen and Prince stayed for four days, keeping the staff on its toes to ensure all needs were met and that proper protocol was followed when serving the royal couple. As a limousine whisked them away at the end of their visit, a smiling President Eisenhower said to West, "If they'd stayed a day or two longer, we'd soon be calling them Liz and Phil."

West was overseeing another state dinner a month later, this time for the King of Monaco, when Mamie called him and asked him to go to the president's room right away. He went upstairs to find the president in his pajamas and robe, sitting on his bed and speaking to his doctor. The president had suffered a stroke. Mamie told West to prepare to cancel the dinner, and as West began to make a list of all that would need to be done to cancel an event of this magnitude, the president said that the dinner would not be cancelled. He agreed to not attend but only if Mamie went in his place. Reluctantly, she agreed, and the president soon recovered.

One of the most awkward occasions that West managed was the visit of Nikita Khrushchev, his wife, his daughter, and his son-in-law in September 1959. It was the height of the Cold War, and this was the first visit to the United States by a Soviet leader. Khrushchev's visit to the U.S. is remembered by many for his anger at being refused the opportunity to see Disneyland due to the security risks that the large crowds would pose. For West and the White House staff, the visit was memorable partly because the Khrushchev family refused to dress formally for the state dinner. The Eisenhowers kept with tradition, anyway, as the president dressed in white tie and Mamie in a ball gown. After an uneasy toast from Khrushchev that was a subtle boast about the Soviet Union, most were glad to see the dinner end and the guests of honor leave.

As Mamie Eisenhower sadly left the White House in 1960, West prepared to work with the newest first lady, Jacqueline Kennedy. The first order of business, to Mamie's horror, was a complete renovation of the White House interior to a style more suitable to the young Kennedys and their children, Caroline and John-John. West now found himself dealing with a more informal, spontaneous household and "thoroughly enjoying the most creative and challenging work to which the chief usher had ever been put."

Unlike Mrs. Eisenhower, Jackie Kennedy did not schedule regular meetings with West. However, he learned to carry a legal pad with him at all times because if he ran into her in the hallway, she may decide to hold a meeting right then and there. She popped into the Usher's Office when ideas struck her and kept no regular schedule other than the hour that she read to her children each night. Dinner was at odd hours and could be anything from grilled cheese sandwiches to an elegant meal of pheasant and vegetables.

In 1962, Jackie famously took America on a televised tour of the White House, broadcast on all three leading networks. She had decided as soon as she knew that her husband was running for president that if he won, the White House would be her project. With an eye toward historic preservation, which required consulting old books and articles on the presidential mansion, Mrs. Kennedy transformed the White House from an old house to a national monument. West could often be seen following the First Lady and two French restoration experts, notebook in hand, to take down her orders for the restoration project. When West informed her that he was running into dealers who wanted to inflate prices on antique rugs that she wanted for the White House, she replied to him in a memo that she was outraged that anyone would try to "gyp" the White House. West was instructed to tell the dealers that they would get a photo in the official guidebook and a tax deduction and if that was not good enough, "goodbye!"

On November 22, 1963, West was home doing his own redecorating when he heard on the radio that President Kennedy had been shot. He immediately left for the White House and by the time he arrived, the president had died. West quickly organized a shocked White House staff: butlers were ordered to make coffee and maids were told to prepare guest rooms while he tried to think of what to do next. Word quickly came to him from Jackie that she wanted the house to be just as it was when Abraham Lincoln lay in state in 1865. West and the staff worked from a reference book from the curator's office to accommodate the first lady's wishes.

Even as the nation prepared to lay the president to rest, the White House was moving out the Kennedy's belongings and preparing for the arrival of Lyndon and Lady Bird Johnson. As Mrs. Kennedy and West stood out on the White House lawn, looking at the trampoline and sandbox, she asked him if he would always be her friend. Unable to speak, he simply nodded in reply. West slept on a couch in the Usher's Office until the Kennedys were moved out and the Johnsons were moved in.

The day after President Kennedy's funeral, Lady Bird Johnson told West that she wanted him to run the White House. She told him that she had run her own house for 30 years and wanted to spend her time on other things. He helped the Johnsons prepare for their sudden move by meeting the new First Lady at her home, armed with blue prints and photos of the White House. They discussed arrangement for the servants – Lady Bird wanted to bring her own – and West assured her that it was acceptable to have her servants on the White House payroll since there were two openings.

The Johnsons were in the White House for five years. West's duties ranged from ensuring that the president's showerhead had the right amount of pressure to planning the wedding of his daughters, Luci and Lynda. He assisted Lady Bird as she picked up where Jackie Kennedy had left off on the White House restoration, intent that the work continue and the presidential mansion be preserved as a national monument. If need be, Lady Bird consulted with Jackie on decisions. The fact that the modern day chief usher has responsibilities in historic preservation stems from the work of Mrs. Kennedy and Mrs. Johnson.

The Johnson daughters certainly changed the energy of the White House. Luci was a teenager when she moved in, and Lynda transferred from the University of Texas to George Washington University after her father became president. West recalled that the second floor often sounded like a girl's dormitory. The third floor solarium was converted to a "dating room," where Luci entertained young Patrick Nugent. At one point, Luci asked West to convert the sliding glass door to wood so that "everybody" could not see what was happening in there. Of course, West understood "everybody" to be her mother. The White House buzzed when Lynda dates the handsome actor George Hamilton.

The president himself was also a significant change for West. Full of energy, LBJ was known to roll up the rug and dance the foxtrot on the marble floor at midnight after his workday was done. West considered the Johnson's the "danciest" family he had ever met, and he took his own turns on the dance floor with them.

West's last day at the White House was March 1, 1969 as Richard and Pat Nixon began their time in the White House. Pat was disappointed when West said he planned to retire. He had come highly recommended by Mamie Eisenhower. Later, West returned as a guest at a dinner celebrating the acquisition of a portrait of James Madison, which Mrs. Johnson had tried hard to acquire. As he went through the receiving line and shook President Nixon's hand, the president said, "After all you have done for this house, you are welcome here anytime."

Stephen W. Rochon

When Admiral Stephen Rochon was recruited for the chief usher position in 2007, he did not even know what the job entailed. In fact, he had never even heard of the job. However, after hearing more about the historical nature of the job duties, especially regarding the historic preservation of the president's home and executive office, Rochon was intrigued. He accepted the invitation to interview and nine interviews later, he was hired, making him the first African American to hold the position. He replaced Gary Walters, who had been chief usher for 20 years.

The New Orleans native's road to chief usher was unconventional, and he brought a background far different than that of the previous chief ushers. The son of a military family, Rochon joined the Coast Guard in 1970. Through a series of promotions gained experience in personnel management, collaboration with other agencies, and strategic planning. He graduated with a bachelor's degree in business from Xavier University in Louisiana and earned a Master of Science in National Resource Strategy from National Defense University in Washington, D.C. Perhaps one of his biggest challenges was as director of personnel in the wake of Hurricane Katrina in 2005. He also helped restore three historic homes that dated back to the turn of the century in New Orleans, and he served as an advisor to several museums.

When Rochon took over the chief usher duties, the nation was more focused on sustainability than at any time in history. With that in mind, Rochon was not only interested in preserving the historical integrity of the White House, but in making it more environmentally friendly. Two of the changes he implemented were transition outdoor lighting to LED and converting the swimming pool to solar heat. He was also responsible for supervising the White House information technology staff, something that previous presidents could not even have dreamed of needing. In 2011, after four years of managing the White House, the highly decorated Rochon resigned to join the Department of Homeland Security.

Angella Reid

It was not until 2011 that the White House hired its first female chief usher. Angella Reid got the call that she would be working with the Obamas just before the holidays, putting her into the role just as the White House's busy season was getting ready to kick off. Her closest friends and family members did not even realize that she was in the running, but a position of this nature calls for discretion.

Her 25 years in hotel management prepared Reid for the position. The Jamaica native got her management degree in Munich, Germany at the prestigious Carl Duisberg Gesellschaft School. Before taking a job at the White House, Reid's career took her to some of the world's most elite hotels in Jamaica, Florida, New York, Connecticut, and Virginia.

Chapter 4: White House Butlers

Butlers are responsible for the food and beverage service for the president, the president's family, and any guests to the White House. Of course, flexibility is required because a butler could certainly be called upon to do a variety of tasks. A well-known photograph taken in June 2009 shows butler Von Everett pumping up basketballs for President Barack Obama. Overseeing all of the butlers is the *maître d'hôtel*, which is akin to the head butler. Typically, there are six or seven butlers on staff. A background in the food and beverage industry is a primary requirement for modern residential staff.

Alonzo Fields

Alonzo Fields planned to be an opera singer or maybe a music teacher. He was born in the all-black community of Lyles Station, Indiana, in 1900. His father was the manager of a general store and his mother ran a boarding house for railroad workers. In 1925, Fields went to Boston to study at the New England Conservatory of Music. While there, he worked as the butler for Dr. Samuel Stratton, the president of the Massachusetts Institute of Technology. As payment for his service, Stratton covered Fields' tuition, but this arrangement came to a tragic and abrupt end when Stratton died in 1931. Legend has it that Stratton was friends with Thomas Edison, and when he heard of Edison's death, Stratton died on the spot.

It was the Great Depression and Fields had a wife and a child to feed. He put aside the idea of a career in music and set his sights on survival. However, it was his music that got his foot in the door of the White House. While working for Stratton, Fields played piano at a party hosted by Stratton and attended by President Herbert Hoover and his wife, Lou Henry. After Stratton died, Lou Henry remembered Fields and invited him to spend a year as a butler at the White House. It was not exactly his dream, but he welcomed the opportunity and took his family to Washington, D.C.

When Fields arrived, the Southerners on staff were skeptical of the man they considered a "Yankee" from the North. In fact, it was assumed that Lou Henry would be put off by Fields' height. The First Lady was known to not approve of tall butlers. However, when the 6'2" Fields arrived, she welcomed him warmly. For Fields, it was the first night of a 21-year career in the White House.

Fields quickly learned that, like most of the nation, the White House was segregated. He was expected to serve the president and his guests, but when it came time for him to eat his own meals, Fields had to eat in a separate dining room with the other black staff members. He said of his feelings at the time, "I'm good enough to handle the president's food and do everything, but I cannot eat with the help." When Franklin and Eleanor Roosevelt moved into the White House, Eleanor hired only black residential staff in an effort to ease the racial tension, eliminating the need for separate dining rooms.

Fields also quickly realized that this was a job that he wanted to keep. Three days after he started working at the White House, he was told to serve Hoover and his Cabinet at the "medicine ball breakfast table." Hoover's doctor invented a game that was designed to help keep the president fit. It was similar to volleyball except that the players heaved a small medicine ball over the net. When the game was over, the president took his breakfast promptly at 6:30 a.m., under the magnolia tree near the South Portico of the White House.

As he served breakfast, Fields realized the magnitude of what he was hearing. Hoover and his Cabinet would discuss the Great Depression and the financial crisis that gripped the nation. After the famed aviator, Charles Lindbergh's baby was kidnapped in 1932, Hoover regularly reviewed the progress toward solving the crime. It was while serving breakfast that Fields first heard of the Democratic senator from New York, Franklin Delano Roosevelt.

Although it is never permissible for a butler to interject into a conversation, Fields could not help but hear them and decided to keep a diary. His father had kept one and Fields thought it was amusing to read entries on events such as Halley's Comet or the sinking of the Titanic. He felt like his own grandchildren might find it interesting someday, so he started keeping a notebook in his pocket. Using his own shorthand and out of the sight of others, Fields would keep notes on events from his day in the White House. The idea of publishing his memoirs never crossed his mind. He could not imagine that anyone would believe or even care what a black man had to say about working in the White House.

When the Roosevelts moved into the White House, life changed for Fields and the rest of the staff. The White House residential staff is there to serve the president and how previous presidents wanted things no longer mattered when administrations changed. The Hoovers were far more formal than the family that lived in the White House from 1933 until 1945. The staff learned to adapt to a more relaxed style of leadership. Out were the seven-course ceremonial dinners– even if it was just President Hoover and the First Lady – and in was an erratic schedule with visitors at all times of the day. The Roosevelt inaugural dinner in 1933 should have been a sign of things to come: scrambled eggs, fried potatoes, bacon and toast, all served on the same plate. Still, even if eggs were on the dinner menu, dinner was served in coat and tails until John and Jackie Kennedy did away with that tradition.

World War II ended the Great Depression but brought with it a new set of issues and concerns. Roosevelt created a "war room," which was previously a billiards room and is now known as the Map Room. The only domestic staff permitted in the war room was Fields. Even though most the world did not know it, FDR was in a wheel chair due to paralysis, caused either by polio or Guillain-Barre Syndrome. Therefore, he needed someone with him at all times, and it was often Fields. While he maintained discretion and confidentiality at all times, Fields was alarmed to here that if needed, the U.S. planned to mobilize police from across the country to Chicago and make that city the last line of defense if Japan invaded from the West. The western half of the U.S. was going to be sacrificed if it came to that. It was this type of information that went into his notebook.

The war also brought a notable visitor to the White House. British Prime Minister Winston Churchill made a famous visit to Washington for two weeks in 1941 and into early 1942. Fields recalled that Churchill was a strong personality with a strong appetite and the Churchill entourage took over the entire East Wing of the White House. Among Fields' duties were to ensure that Churchill had his favorites food and drink during the course of his stay. A typical breakfast would be eggs, bacon, or ham, cold cuts with mustard, two types of fruit, orange juice, a tumbler of sherry, and a pot of tea.

Fields also arranged for Churchill to have his customary two Scotch and sodas with lunch, French champagne with dinner, 90 year-old brandy after dinner, and more Scotch and soda before bed. Churchill was known to keep late hours and Fields stayed as long as Churchill was awake, in case he needed something. When Churchill rang for Fields because he had run out of Scotch, he told Fields he was not sure about him. When Fields asked how he could be of service, Churchill told him to be sure to say that he was a teetotaler if anyone every asked. "I'll defend you to the last drop," Fields replied.

Of all the presidents that Fields served, his best relationship was with Roosevelt's successor, Harry Truman. Harry and Bess Truman were different from the Roosevelts. Franklin and Eleanor were not alone in the White House once and rarely, if ever, had a private dinner with the two of them. Their marriage was one of political convenience by this time as Eleanor was aware of her husband's extramarital affair with Lucy Mercer. The Trumans, while reserved with their feelings in the typical Midwestern way, did nearly everything together, whether it was eat, read, or listen to the radio. One of their evening rituals was to have a cocktail together. Fields prepared their drinks but his first few tries at making their old fashioneds did not go well. Bess thought they were too sweet and complained to J.B. West. She said they were the worst she had ever tasted. Fields, his ego hurting a bit, prepared the First Lady a double bourbon on the rocks one night and stood by while she tasted it. She smiled, voiced her approval and said that was the way the Trumans liked their old fashioneds.

Fields came to have a terrific deal of respect for the Trumans. The president took the time to know the names of all of the staff members and introduced them by name to guests, something that had never been done before. Truman also knew what was happening in their personal lives and took an interest in their families. He was also the first president since Calvin Coolidge to go into the kitchen. Coolidge had gone in to make sure that the staff was not giving away too much food. Truman went there to thank Elizabeth Moore, the head cook, for baking him a birthday cake on the night that Germany surrendered in World War II. Fields said of Truman that he respected Fields "as a man, not as a servant to be tolerated." Roosevelt was friendly but was an aristocrat at heart and could not understand common men the way that Truman did. As for Bess, Fields found her a good person to work for because she accepted no flattery and nobody who shirked their responsibilities. If you did your best, Fields believed that there was nobody more understanding than Bess Truman

It was Truman that gave Fields the promotion to *maître d'hôtel,* or the equivalent of the chief butler, in charge of about 15 staff members. He was the first African American to hold that position. He earned that promotion on the strength of his homemade biscuits. Bess did not care much for Washington and especially missed the fresh bread and rolls of Missouri. The president told Fields this and Fields promised that she would have fresh rolls the next night for dinner. However, when Fields told the kitchen staff, they said they had too much to do already, so Fields bought the ingredients himself and baked the rolls for the first lady. He watched as she ate the fresh rolls with butter with pleasure and the next day the president told him that she was so happy with what he had done that he was going to be promoted. He was responsible for making menu suggestions for important teas, receptions, state dinners and family dinners, all subject to approval from the first lady. Fields had to keep track of hundreds of pieces of napkins, silverware, and dishes. The chefs and servers reported directly to him.

As the maître d', Fields was called upon to put together a last minute dinner on a Sunday in June 1950. The Trumans were back home in Missouri, so the White House kitchen was closed. Thinking that they would not be needed, Fields sent much of the staff home for the weekend. However, he got word that the president was returning to the White House that evening and that he should start preparing dinners and cocktails at 8 p.m. With the help of the Washington Police Department, residential staff was called in to help prepare the dinner.

In the cab on the way to the White House, Felds planned the dinner, based on what he already had on hand, just as anyone would. Knowing the president's preferences for comfort food in times of crisis, Fields prepared a menu of fried chicken breast, potatoes, gravy, buttered asparagus, and hot biscuits. Vanilla ice cream and chocolate sauce was served for dessert. When he arrived, he set the table, started cooking, and made canapés until the cook arrived at 6 p.m. The first butler arrived at 7:45 p.m., five minutes before General Omar Bradley and Secretary of State Dean Acheson. When Truman arrived at 8:30, the dinner began, and he and the guests began discussion on U.S. involvement in the crisis is Korea.

When Truman left office, he gave Fields two parting gifts. One was a black fedora, of the style Truman was often known to wear. Fields' widow gave the hat to the mayor of Medford, Massachusetts as a gift to the city in 2008. The hat was handmade by Lees Fifth Avenue in New York and is inscribed "Honorable Harry Truman." The other gift was the famous sign in the Oval Office reading "The Buck Stops Here," although the White House staff knew that the buck truly stopped with Bess.

Fields left the White House in 1953, shortly after Dwight and Mamie Eisenhower moved into the White House. His first wife was ill, and he returned to Massachusetts to be closer to her. After he retired in 1960, Fields wrote his memoirs, *My 21 Years in the White House*, which has provided invaluable insight into the inner workings of the White House. At the age of 80 and now a widower, Fields married an old flame from the past, 62 year-old Mayland McLaughlin. Alonzo Fields died in Cambridge on March 23, 1994 at the age of 93.

Eugene Allen

When Eugene Allen learned about an opening at the White House, it was 1952, Truman was president, and much of the South was still in the grips of Jim Crow. The young African American from Virginia was not looking for a job but followed up on the lead, anyway, and went to the White House to meet with Alonzo Fields. Fields liked Allen and offered him a job as the pantry man for $2,400 a year. As the pantry man, Allen was responsible for washing dishes, stacking the silverware, and keeping the cabinets well stocked. Little did Allen realize that he would go on to work for eight presidential families, ending with Ronald and Nancy Reagan.

Allen met many dignitaries in his 50 years at the White House. One of the most memorable was Martin Luther King, Jr. King asked to meet the residential staff, and when he saw Allen, he complimented him on his tuxedo. Whether it was serving warm milk to Lyndon Johnson while protestors on the White House lawn gave him a nervous stomach or drinking root beer with Jimmy Carter, Allen was loyal to all of the presidents and their families.

Allen's tenure in the White House began as the Civil Rights Movement was heating up. He was in Washington when the Supreme Court ruled on *Brown vs. Board of Education* in 1954 and desegregated public schools. He was there when Eisenhower sent in the 101st Airborne to guard the Little Rock Nine. He was there for the March on Washington in 1963 and for President Kennedy's assassination months later. He was actually invited to attend the funeral but declined, saying that somebody had to stay back at the White House and receive visitors. Still, his son, Charles recalled that the day that Kennedy was shot, Allen pulled his coat on to return to work, he suddenly fell against the wall and burst into tears. It was the only time Charles remembered seeing his father cry.

Allen was in Washington when President Lyndon Johnson signed the Civil Rights Act of 1964, although he was also there to hear the southern man's racially charged vulgarities.

As the Civil Rights Movement progressed and Black Power gained a foothold, many younger African Americans questioned the notion of a man like Allen working as a butler. It perpetuated stereotypes, they said. Allen still took pride in his work and in 1980, he was promoted to maître d. As the years passed, he noticed that African Americans were getting more powerful positions in government. Colin Powell and Condoleezza Rice were both appointed secretary of state. The idea of a black president seemed closer, but neither he nor his wife thought they would live to see it.

One of Allen's greatest honors was when Nancy Reagan told him that he would not be working the evening of a state dinner for German Chancellor Helmut Kohl. Allen was concerned as he waited for the explanation: he and his wife, Helene, were invited guests. Allen recalled the odd but enjoyable experience of being served the champagne that he had personally stacked in the kitchen by butlers he had trained. He is believed to be the only butler ever invited to a state dinner at the White House.

Allen retired in 1986. Twenty-two years later, he and his wife prepared to vote for Barack Obama and help make him the first black president. However, Helene died the night before the election. Allen voted without her. Weeks later, Allen received an invitation to Obama's inauguration and tears filled his eyes as a Marine escorted him to his seat. When Allen died in 2010, Stephen Rochon read a letter from the president. Obama commended him for his service and his "abiding patriotism." When Allen was laid to rest, he was dressed in a suit with white gloves and a White House pin attached to his lapel.

Chapter 5: Other Residential Staff

Executive Chef

For many years, the White House kitchen was staffed by slaves and later by African American domestic help. After that, caterers or Navy stewards supplied the White House meals and neither was known to provide the most palatable food in Washington. It was not until Jackie Kennedy hired French chef, Rene Verdon, in 1961 that the White House had a full-time executive chef. Today, the executive chef reports to the chief usher and oversees all three White House kitchens and supervises four sous chefs. The executive chef is typically appointed by each administration.

The executive chef does not get complete control over menus but does offer suggestions. Desserts and pastries are handled exclusively by the executive pastry chef. In 2005, Chris Comerford became the first female to have the job when she was selected after a lengthy interview process. She was already an assistant chef, which may have given her a leg up since she already knew how to prepare huevos rancheros the way the president liked them, but she still had to prove herself. Each chef in the running had to prepare tasting menu for George and Laura Bush. Before joining the White House staff, Comerford earned a bachelor's degree in food technology in her native Philippines, and then worked in Austria and hotels in the U.S.

Grounds Superintendent

It is not just the interior of the White House than needs to be managed. The area surrounding the White House is officially called "President's Park" and covers 18 and a half acres. This includes the North and South lawns, the Rose Garden, the Jacqueline Kennedy Garden, and in the Obama White House, Michelle Obama's vegetable garden. It is the first vegetable garden planted at the White House since Eleanor Roosevelt's victory garden. There are 500 trees and 4,000 shrubs. Some of the grounds are private, such as the Garden Sanctuary, but a significant portion of the ground are public. Press conferences and departure and arrival ceremonies are often held on the White House grounds. Easter egg rolls, t-ball games, concerts, and 4th of July picnics have all taken place on the White House grass.

It has taken two centuries of maintenance and deliberate planning to create the lush grounds that surround the White House. Throughout those two centuries, hundreds of staff have tended to the mowing, trimming, planting, and harvesting. Thomas Jefferson hired the first White House gardener. First Lady Edith Wilson ordered that sheep be put on the grass so that they could graze and reduce some of the manpower needed. In 1972, Dale Haney began working at the White House as a gardener. He is still there today only now he is the superintendent of all grounds, supervising a staff of 20, which includes electricians, gardeners, and maintenance workers. Haney and his staff are all employees of the National Park Service. Just as the staff inside the house must prepare the interior to receive visitors, Haney and his crew are busy every day making sure that the grounds are a proper reflection of the president's home. Simply mowing the North and South lawns takes eight hours.

Managing the grounds is not the only responsibility that has fallen to Haney. For 40 years, he has served as the unofficial dog walker when the president's family is away. Haney, who finds that many people are more interested in the president's dog than the president, has tended to presidential pets since the Nixon administration. Even on a normal day, the presidential dogs can be seen trailing after the groundskeepers as they go about their daily activities.

Social Secretary

While the chief usher oversees the White House as a whole, the social secretary is specifically responsible for event management. That includes determining guest lists, seating arrangements, menus, and anything else that is required to host a dinner or throw a party. Given the number of events that can occur at the White House, it is a busy job that requires tact, discretion, and the ability to juggle many tasks at once. The social secretary for Calvin Coolidge, Mary Randolph, said of the position's qualifications, "The White House Secretary should combine keen perceptions and sensibilities with the strength of Hercules, the hide of a rhinoceros, great endurance, and a sense of humor."

The first social secretary was appointed in 1901. Isabella Hagner, First Lady Edith Roosevelt's executive clerk. Prior to that time, only men had been responsible for keeping social lists but Mrs. Roosevelt was a strong advocate for Hagner, and, after a rather public controversy, Hagner was given the job. Teddy Roosevelt's administration is remembered for being far more glamorous and focused on entertainment than any administration before it, making a social secretary a necessity. Future administrations continued to utilize clerks and secretaries in this role until the social secretary became an official position in the White House staff during the Eisenhower administration.

There has been no set path to getting the social secretary job. Like many of the key staff positions, many who have had the job did not apply for it. They happened to be in the right place at the right time. In February 2011, Jeremy Bernard became the first male social secretary when he was appointed by the Obama administration. He became known to President Obama when he helped raise tens of millions of dollars for Obama's 2008 campaign.

For Bernard, the role of social secretary has evolved well beyond the days of making sure that place settings are appropriate to the occasion, although that is still part of the job. He is not only for coordinating some of the most complex events that the White House has ever seen, he has brought fundraising to the position. Bernard, who is gay, paved the way for some of the nation's wealthiest gay Democrats to write checks in support of Obama's 2012 campaign. In a sight common only to the Obama White House, openly gay couples were seen comfortably mingling and posing for photographers at a state dinner for British Prime Minister David Cameron. The welcoming atmosphere is largely attributed to Bernard's influence.

Many of the former social secretaries have formed a tightknit group of alumni and Bernard has been accepted with open arms. He took the time to visit an assisted living center to meet with Letitia Baldrige, Jackie Kennedy's social secretary, and learned tricks of the trade while chatting over French wine. Her best piece of advice to Bernard was to "keep his mouth shut." After Desiree Rogers was fired for allowing two reality show contestant to crash a White House event in 2009, sparking a national controversy, the White House was ready for a social secretary who could perform the duties while keeping a low profile. After Bernard hosted a luncheon at the White House for the former social secretaries and presented them all with a bouquet of roses, one of them remarked that Bernard suits the role perfectly and "he just gets it."

Bibliography

Benac, Nancy. "New White House Usher Angella Reid Comes from Hotel Industry." Huffington Post. October 24, 2011. http://www.huffingtonpost.com/2011/10/24/new-white-house-usher-ang_n_1028303.html

Bumiller, Elizabeth. "White Gloves Not Needed." *The New York Times.* April 20, 2012. http://www.nytimes.com/2012/04/22/style/jeremy-bernard-white-house-social-secretary-makes-his-mark.html?pagewanted=all&_r=0

C-SPAN. *A Day in the Life of the White House Chief Usher.* Film. http://whitehouse.c-span.org/Video/WhiteHouseStaff/DayofWhiteHouse-Chief-Usher.aspx.

C-SPAN. *White House Gardens and Grounds.* Film. http://whitehouse.c-span.org/Video/ArtGallery/GardenAndGround.aspx

C-SPAN. *Interviews with White House Staff.* Film. http://whitehouse.c-span.org/Video/WhiteHouseStaff.aspx

Fields, Alonzo. *My 21 Years in the White House.* New York: Fawcett. 1961.

Haygood, Wil. "A Butler Well Served by this Election." *Washington Post.* November 7, 2008. http://articles.washingtonpost.com/2008-11-07/politics/36906532_1_white-house-black-man-history

Hoover, Irwin. *Forty-two Years in the White House.* New York: Houghlin Mifflin. 1934.

Taylor, Elizabeth Dowling. *A Slave in the White House: Paul Jennings and the Madisons.* New York: MacMillian. 2012.

West, J.B. *Upstairs at the White House: My Life with the First Ladies.* New York: Warner. 1973.

White House Historical Association. "The White House Social Secretary: Welcoming the World to the President's House."
http://www.whitehousehistory.org/whha_shows

Made in the USA
Middletown, DE
15 August 2020